Truly Foul & Cheesy™

Tudors
Facts
& Jokes

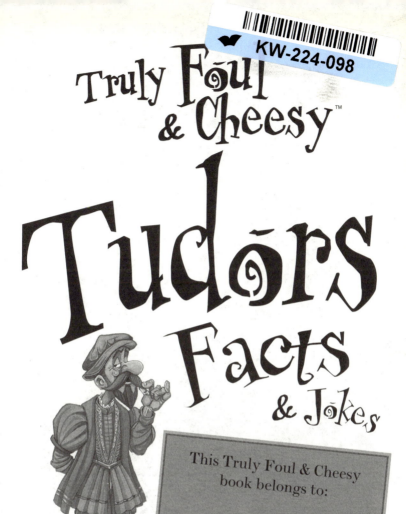

This Truly Foul & Cheesy
book belongs to:

....

Written by

John Townsend

Illustrated by

David Antram

BOOK HOUSE
a SALARIYA imprint

Introduction

Warning – reading this book might not make you LOL (laugh out loud) but it could make you GOL (groan out loud), feel sick out loud or SEL (scream even louder). If you are reading this in a library by a SILENCE sign... get ready to be thrown out!

4

Truly Foul & Cheesy™
& Cheesy

Tudors

Facts & Jokes

sup

<

Published in Great Britain in MMXIX by
Book House, an imprint of
The Salariya Book Company Ltd
25 Marlborough Place, Brighton BN1 1UB
www.salariya.com

ISBN: 978-1-912537-87-7

SALARIYA
SCRIBO BOOK HOUSE SCRIBBLERS

1 3 5 7 9 8 6 4 2

A CIP catalogue record for this book is available
from the British Library.

Printed and bound in China.
Printed on paper from sustainable sources.

Created and designed by
David Salariya.

Visit
www.salariya.com
for our online catalogue and
free fun stuff.

PAPER FROM
SUSTAINABLE
FORESTS

Author:
John Townsend worked as a
secondary school teacher before
becoming a full-time writer.
He specialises in illuminating and
humorous information books for
all ages.

Artist:
David Antram studied at
Eastbourne College of Art and then
worked in advertising for 15 years
before becoming a full-time artist.
He has illustrated many children's
non-fiction books.

Disclaimer: the author really hasn't made anything up in this book (apart from some daft limericks and jokes). He checked out the foul facts as best he could and even double-checked the fouler bits to make sure – so please don't get too upset if you find out something different from a Tudor ghost, an executioner with a sharp axe or a royal Groom of the Stool (you'll soon find out what that is, if you dare).

If I had my way, I'd RATify the lot!

5

Official warning

Tudor life was often harsh and short. Apart from wealthy Tudors, most people would expect to die before they were 40 years old. About one in three children died by the time they were 10 years old. And the good news was, if you were a girl and made it to 12 years old, you could get married (it was 14 for boys). As for what food, entertainment, punishments and diseases a Tudor could expect to meet in a day... do you really want to know? Be prepared to be disgusted as the foul and cheesy Tudor facts coming up are enough to make you cringe. Brace yourself – you have been warned...

Historians are still finding out all sorts of foul and cheesy facts about life 500 years ago during Tudor times. That was a period in British history lasting over 100 years when the Tudor royal family was in charge of England and Wales – and what a colourful bunch they were. Meanwhile, the Stuarts ruled Scotland and, of course, there were often big rows between them all. There was a lot going on between 1485 and 1603, when all kinds of ideas were taking shape, lots of discoveries were being made and yes… plenty of scary things were going on, too.

Loopy limerick

Your life as a poor Tudor peasant
Could often be grossly unpleasant,
While rich people chewed
On meatier food
Like a partridge stuffed in a roast pheasant.

(Yes, a multi-bird roast with
smaller birds stuffed in larger ones
was the ultimate Tudor dining
experience.)

How to think like a Tudor...

These are genuine Tudor riddles (warning –
they're not very funny!

Q: What is it that never was and never will be?
A: A mouse's nest in a cat's ear. (Hmm – it was
    probably the way they told it that was hilarious.)

Q: What is it that never freezeth?
A: Boiling water.

Q: What beast is it that hath
    her tail between her eyes?
A: It is a cat when she licketh
    her behind.

Royal reminder

Tudor kings and queens were all-powerful, but also nervy, fearing enemies everywhere about to strike (which they often were). The royal Tudor soap opera was full of extreme characters, so let's meet the cast list:

Ruler	Length of reign
Henry VII	1485–1509
Henry VIII	1509–1547
Edward VI	1547–1553
Lady Jane Grey	1553 – 9 days
Mary I	1553–1558
Elizabeth I	1558–1603

The start of the Tudors

Life in Britain 550 years ago was full of fights. There was civil war about who should be running the country – the reds or the whites? (The red rose was the symbol of the House of Lancaster and the white rose was the House of York). For over 30 years, battles between them raged on. In 1457 a baby called Henry was born in the 'red camp' (2 months after Edmund Tudor, his father, died).

Henry Tudor was born in Wales when his mother, Margaret, was only thirteen. He was later to become the only Welsh boy ever to be king of England. Henry Tudor belonged to the Lancaster branch of the Plantagenet Royal Family (fighting the House of York, in the Wars of the Roses). Each branch wanted control of the English throne and it all came to a head in a battle in 1485. Henry marched across Wales to attack King Richard III at the Battle of Bosworth Field in Leicestershire. King Richard was killed – so Henry Tudor was crowned King Henry VII and the Tudor period began. It lasted for the next 118 years.

Limerick

The Lancaster lad, Henry Tudor,
Met a nice girl of York and pursued her.
They soon became wed
And their youngest son said
'As king I'll be shrewder and ruder.'
And he was (Henry VIII).

To patch up all those quarrels between York and Lancaster, Henry married Elizabeth of York (the niece of Richard III, so the family wedding must have been interesting!). The king and queen had 4 children: Arthur (who died aged 15), Margaret, Henry and Katherine (who died at birth, together with mother Elizabeth on her 37th birthday in 1503).

Tudor drama

Flashback to Richmond Palace, near London, 1502. King Henry VII sends for his son...

Henry Tudor: Come here, son – we need to talk.

Henry Junior: What about, dad? I fancy some chips.

Henry Tudor: Don't talk daft. Potatoes haven't been discovered yet. Haven't you read page 64?

Henry Junior: No wonder I'm hungry. I'm a growing lad.

Henry Tudor: You're telling me. You eat like a horse.

Henry Junior: Rubbish – I've never eaten hay and sugar lumps haven't been invented.

16

Henry Tudor: We must discuss the future. I'm an old man now, I'm 46. Your brother Arthur has now died, and he was only 15.

Henry Junior: And his wife is very upset. They'd been married for under 6 months and she hasn't opened all the wedding presents yet.

Henry Tudor: That's why I want to talk. I'd like you to be Catherine's next present.

Henry Junior: How do you mean, dad?

Henry Tudor: You'll need to marry her. She's from Aragon in Spain so if you marry her it will help our country's friendship with Spain. Look, here she comes now.

Catherine: Hola, Henry.

Henry Junior: Hi, Catherine – will you marry me?

Catherine: Qué?

Henry Junior: The thing is, dad – I'm only 11.

Henry Tudor: You'll grow. Eat another swan for breakfast. I want you to be king after me. You already have my first name and middle name.

Henry Junior: Middle name?

Henry Tudor: Yes – 'the'. I'm Henry the seventh. You'll be Henry the eighth. And your son will be Henry the ninth.

Henry Junior: What if I don't have a son?

Henry Tudor: What? Don't even go there. You must. You've got to have a strong heir.

Henry Junior: What if my hair falls out? Catherine doesn't look very happy. It looks like she's chewed a wasp. Ha ha – get it?

Henry Tudor: What are you on about?

Henry Junior: Chewed-a... Tudor. Get it? That's so funny. I love chistes cursis.

Henry Tudor: You what?

Henry Junior: That's Spanish for cheesy jokes.

Catherine: Doh!

Lo and behold, they married when Henry Junior was 17, after his father died in 1509.

Henry VII was king for 23 years and he died aged 52 years (a good age in Tudor times). It was Henry Tudor's youngest son who took over the Tudor Crown next, becoming one of England's most notorious kings.

Mighty Henry

King Henry VIII (1491–1547) and Catherine of Aragon had a baby girl called Mary. Henry wasn't happy because he wanted a son to become the next Tudor king. He blamed his wife for not having a boy so he decided to divorce her and get another wife. The Pope (the head of the Catholic Church) said he couldn't do that. Henry wasn't going to be told what to do so he made himself the head of the Church in England. Now he could do what he liked!

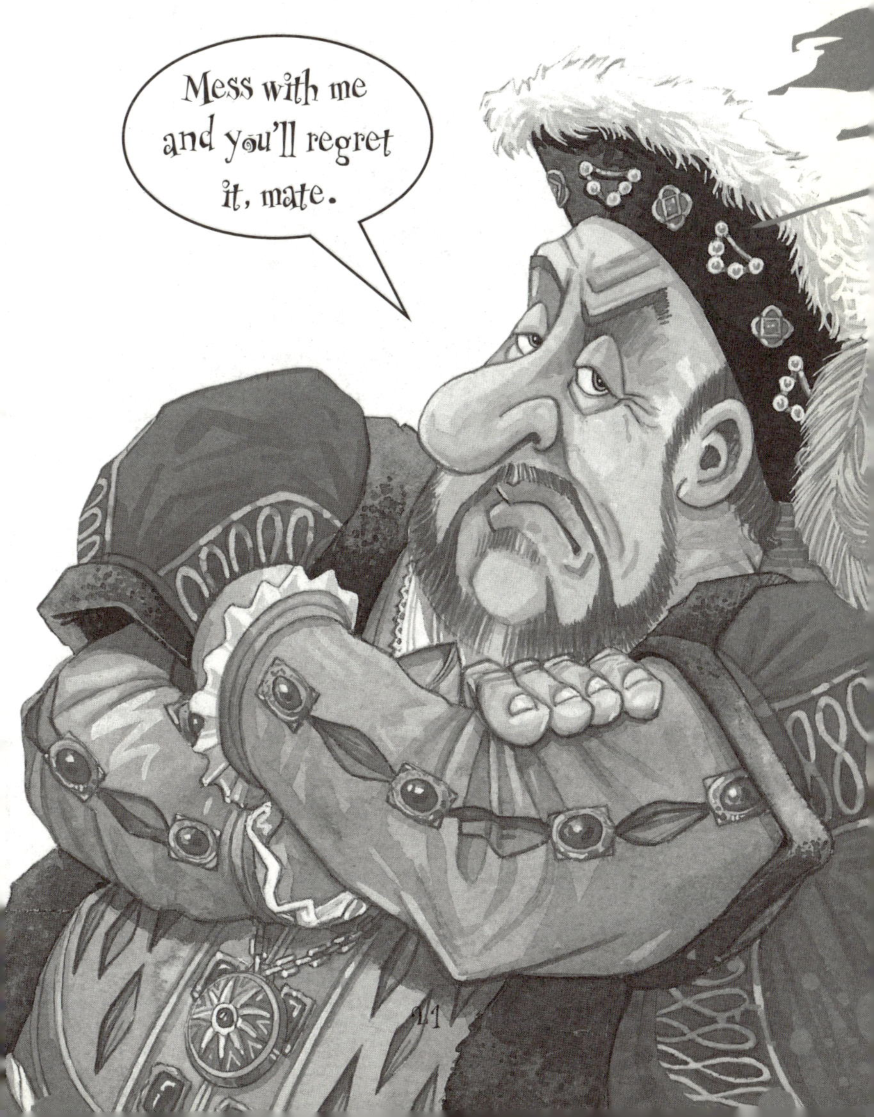
Mess with me
and you'll regret
it, mate.

Wife Number Two

King Henry married Anne Boleyn and anyone who dared to disagree was executed for treason (which was basically anything the king didn't like). When Anne gave birth to a baby daughter (Elizabeth), you can imagine what Henry said. 'Time for another wife.'

Anne Boleyn was only 29 when Henry decided to get rid of her. He accused her of all sorts (like being a witch). In 1536 Anne was taken to Tower Green at the Tower of London. She slowly climbed up all the steps to the scaffold to meet her executioner dressed in black. Anne spoke to the invited audience before kneeling with a blindfold. The executioner raised his sword and beheaded her with one blow. Legend has it that her lips were still moving when he lifted her head from the straw. They were probably saying 'ouch'.

Wife Number Three

Henry married Jane Seymour just 11 days after Anne's execution. Now he hoped to have a son, rather than his two daughters (he didn't think girls would be any good to take over from him). At last, baby Edward was born, but Jane died shortly afterwards and heartbroken Henry soon began looking for another wife.

Time for verse

Wife Number Four

Henry took three years and then
He got engaged – an Anne again.
1540 – when, thick as thieves,
Henry married Anne of Cleves.
Another marriage few endorsed...
Within six months they were divorced.

Wife Number Five

In days he'd wed another queen;
Him forty-nine and her nineteen.
Catherine Howard was her name,
But then the accusations came.
Her ways old Henry disapproved,
And so, he had her head removed.
1542 – Catherine beheaded.

Wife Number Six

Within a year, how most bizarre,
He married a young Katherine Parr.
With eyebrows raised, the deed was done,
Him over fifty, she thirty-one.

King Henry VIII somehow contrived
To six wives he'd be wedded.
The third one died, the sixth survived,
Two divorced, and two beheaded.
Or if you'd prefer…
Divorced, beheaded, died, divorced,
beheaded, survived.

Cheesy pun

King Henry and his wives moved into our street. They lived Tudors down.

Big and grumpy

As King Henry VIII grew older, larger and even grumpier, all around him had to beware. He sent more men and women to their deaths than any other monarch – probably well over 50,000 people. Anyone who disobeyed could be arrested for treason and executed. Yikes!

Limerick time

All Tudors risked plenty of danger
When Henry grew older and stranger...
Especially his wives
Would fear for their lives;
Each knew, with an axe, he'd
exchange her.
(And be heading off to rearrange her.)

Foul alert...

If Henry's foul temper wasn't bad enough, his smell was probably foul, too.
A quick peep into the king's bathroom…
Henry VIII bathed at Hampton Court (one of his palaces in England) with heated water pumped in from a stove in the next room. As he grew fatter with old age, his legs gave way and he had to be carried to his bath. To ease the pain in his sore legs, his bathwater contained a mixture of herbs, petals and a smelly substance from the rear end of a civet cat from Asia. Believe it or not, this pongy oil was an exotic ingredient in Tudor perfumes, so it probably didn't smell too catty (or Henry might have attracted all the cats from around Hampton Court). Even so, his bedroom must have whiffed to high heaven.

Did you know?

King Henry VIII had someone to help him go to the toilet! At least, he created the job of Groom of the Stool, which was a top job in his court (as well as a bottom one).

The word 'Stool' referred to a portable toilet which was always carried around, along with water, towels and a wash bowl. The Groom of the Stool would have to monitor the king's diet and mealtimes, then organise the day around the king's expected 'motions'. Such an intimate job keeping an eye on the king's bodily functions and washing arrangements was a highly trusted position. What could be more important than making sure soft fabrics for wiping the royal bottom were always close at hand? (Rather than the usual soggy leaves used for commoners' behinds.)

For the royal staff, Hampton Court had a 'great house of easement' with 28 toilet seats on two different levels. This emptied into drains, which carried raw sewage into the River Thames. A team of small boys called 'gong scourers' cleaned these royal toilets by crawling along the drains and scrubbing as they went (more like 'pong-scourers').

The royal wee

Tudor people (royals included) would 'pluck a rose' as they might call it (have a wee) anywhere that looked suitable – in fireplaces, corners of rooms or often in the street. In Edinburgh, people could hire a bucket with a tent-like cloak over it to use as a portable toilet – the first portaloo.

Anyone for a Tudor tinkle?

King-sized appetite

As a young man, Henry was active, athletic and skilled at jousting. A leg injury from jousting later led to big problems and he could no longer exercise. He became much bigger and heavier, especially when his massive meals were full of pork, game, rabbit, peacocks and swans – washed down with plenty of ale (averaging 5,000 calories a day). King Henry's last set of armour showed his waist measured a hefty 147 to 152 centimetres (58 to 60 inches), with his weight being about 140 kilograms (around 22 stone).

Henry's last limerick

One morning, King Henry the Eighth
Declared 'I am Henry the Great-th'
Then he sat up in bed (king-size)
Which collapsed as he said,
'I'm more like King Henry the Weighth!'
(So he died with a heavy heart – and
a heavy everything.)

36

In 1547 Henry **VIII** died at the age of 55. His son Edward (aged 9 years and not a healthy lad) took over as king, but died after just six years.

Edward's first and last limerick...

Aged nine, poor little King Eddie
Was just a wee lad and unready
To become the new king
And the terrible thing,
The crown was unsteady on his heady
(Soon Eddie was already deady).

The next few weeks got very messy...

Lady Jane Grey was next on the throne – Queen of England for just nine days. Lady Jane Grey was the great niece of Henry VIII and on his deathbed, Edward VI named her as his successor to the English throne. So, on 9th July 1553, three days after Edward VI's death, Lady Jane Grey was informed that she was Queen of England. She went to the Tower of London and was officially crowned.

But royal advisors wanted Henry's daughter Mary to be queen. They accused Lady Jane of treason and declared Mary as queen. So, what should become of the 17-year-old Jane? Simple – these were Tudor times. Lady Jane Grey and her husband were beheaded in 1554 and her father was killed a week later. (Three heads are always better than one.)

Cue for a limerick...

What sadness was Lady Jane Grey's,
Who reigned for just nine troubled days.
Her short royal time
Was cut in its prime...
'To the bone,' would seem an apt phrase.

Mary Tudor
(1516-1558)

Queen Mary I of England was the daughter of King Henry VIII and his first wife, Catherine of Aragon. Mary reigned as Queen of England for five gruesome years from 1553 until her death in 1558. Catholics and Protestants were squabbling more than ever and Mary made things even worse. She was a Catholic and put many Protestants to death, which is why she was called Bloody Mary. When she died (possibly from flu, aged 42), her half-sister, Elizabeth, became queen (a Protestant).

Limerick

If Henry the Eighth was dead scary,
Then so was his daughter, Queen Mary.
Whatever you did,
She'd order, 'Get rid.'
So everyone had to be wary.

Elizabeth I (1533–1603)

Queen Elizabeth was the daughter of Anne Boleyn and Henry VIII. She was Queen of England from 1558 to 1603 and in all that time, hundreds of people were executed – many of them women accused of being witches (more of such superstitions yet to come).

Elizabeth packed her wardrobes with more than 2,000 beautiful dresses, all in rich, colourful fabrics. She always wanted more and when she saw Lady Mary Howard, one of her maids of honour, wearing a striking gown, the queen was so jealous that she stole it for herself. What she wanted, she got!

Queen Elizabeth was also known for swearing a lot and her foul language was something she apparently inherited from her father – as well as executing people, like her own cousin from Scotland.

Mary Queen of Scots
(1542-1587)

This Mary (not to be confused with her cousin, Bloody Mary) was Queen of Scotland but she wanted to be Queen of England, too. Unfortunately for her, the job was already taken by her cousin Elizabeth. Eventually, after spending a total of nineteen years as a prisoner on the orders of Queen Elizabeth, Mary Queen of Scots was led to the chopping block in 1587.

Gross alert

Mary's execution wasn't a clean cut. It took three chops before Mary's head fell to the floor. The axeman held her head up for all to see, shouted 'God save the Queen!' and dropped it. He was left holding her wig as her head fell and rolled across the floor. It wasn't one of his best days – nor Mary's, either.

Grisly limerick

The last Tudor Queen, known as Bessie,
Was what you might call 'very dressy',
With her flaming red hair
And incredible flair...
If you crossed her, your neck could get messy.

Squabbles and tiffs

The kings and queens of Europe were forever falling out with each other – often because of religion. Many people and governments joined the new Protestant Church, while others kept faithful to the Catholic Church. That meant big rows, especially in Britain. Just for the record:

- Henry VIII split the English Church away from the Pope in a big row about power. Even so, Henry remained a Catholic to the end of his life.

- Henry's son, Edward VI, was a Protestant.

- Mary I tried to strengthen the Catholic Church – Protestants who disagreed were persecuted.

- Elizabeth I did the opposite and persecuted Catholics. By the end of her reign England was a Protestant country.

- Elizabeth wanted change and liked new inventions. Her time was flush with them. In 1596, Sir John Harington invented the first water closet with a proper flush. He built one in his house which Queen Elizabeth I (his godmother) used with glee – and no doubt with a Groom of the Stool looking on. She was so impressed that she had a 'john' built at Richmond Palace.

Elizabethan verse

All feared a merciless outburst
From Queen Elizabeth the First.
Her tendency for fits of rage
(Just like her dad) was hard to gauge.
Yet still today, her reputation
Has power to stir the British nation.
Under her inspiring reign
The country won its fights with Spain.

The end of an era

Queen Elizabeth I died of old age, in 1603. She had proved to the world that a queen on the English throne could be powerful and respected by many. With her death, the Tudor dynasty came to an end, as she had no children to follow her. It was Queen Mary's son (King James VI of Scotland) who became king next – as James I of England.

With me, you get two kings for the price of one.

By the way, it wasn't just British royals who could be brutal in Tudor times…

Meanwhile, over in Hungary (look away now if you can't stand the sight of blood), Countess Elizabeth Báthory (1560–1614) lived in a very nice castle where she hoped to stay looking young. She thought that bathing in the blood of young women and drinking it would keep her skin gorgeous. It seems she kidnapped and killed over 600 peasants. When her crimes were discovered in 1610, she was put in prison where she later died. She made the Tudor royals look like saints.

More gruesome endings

In the 16th century, 9 out of 10 people died before the age of 40. Over 10% of babies died before their first birthday, and many women died having babies. Dying from disease, starvation and punishments were all risks. So were accidents when people didn't bother about health and safety. Historians have found many records of gross deaths. Here goes...

Death by poo

In 1523, a Cambridge baker named George Duncan went out to his back garden to use the cesspit (a polite way of saying he sat on a wooden seat over a pit of sewage to relieve himself). Alas, he slipped, fell in and drowned in the deadly pooey stench.

Death by bacon

A servant called Elizabeth Browne was warming herself by the kitchen fire in the winter of 1543 when four large pig carcasses hanging in the chimney to smoke fell on her. (Smoking meat preserved it as there were no fridges.) The rope holding the carcasses broke and they crushed the poor woman to death.

Death by rat poison

In Tudor times, people often used arsenic known as ratsbane to kill mice and rats scurrying around their houses. Having deadly poison in the kitchen is never wise. Barbara Gilbert of Leicestershire thought the arsenic powder was flour, so she whisked it up in milk and popped it into her baking. When she tasted her dish, it was just a tad deadly. End of Barbara.

Death by bear

Bears were used in Tudor
entertainment – often cruelly.
There were performing bears
that were made to 'dance' and
others used in bear-baiting, where
dogs and bears fought while
spectators placed bets. Sometimes
bears escaped. You wouldn't
want to come face to face with
a frightened or injured bear.
Agnes Rapte was killed by Lord
Bergavenny's bear when it broke
loose at his house in Kent in 1563.
Another bear bit a man to death in
Oxford in 1565 and was then taken
to live in the royal bear garden to
entertain the royals. Surely Queen
Elizabeth didn't walk up the
garden path with a bear behind?

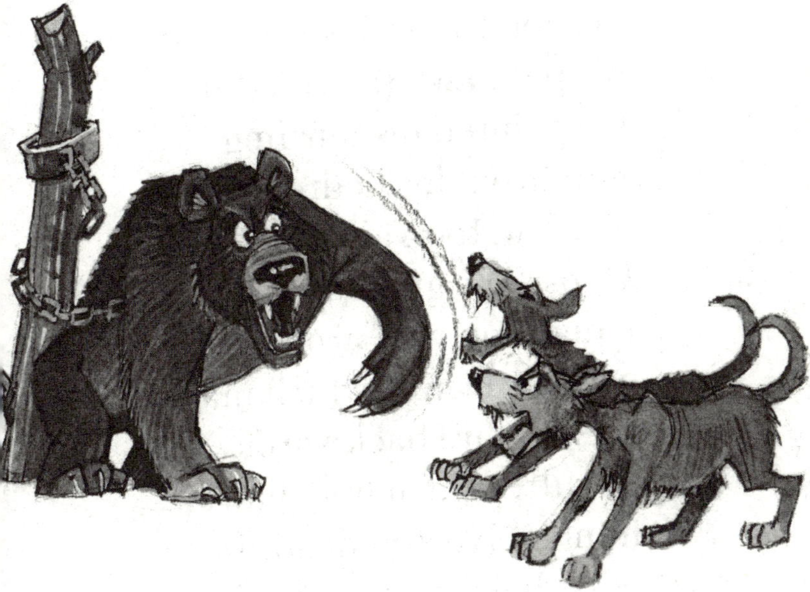

Death by window

In 1599 John Norton
needed to catch supper for
his pet hawk (as you do).
He pointed his 'birding
gun' from his bedroom
window, took aim and fired.
Oops. The gun's spring
caught on wire around the
window frame, which made
the gun fire backwards.
Result: pigeon fine, hawk
hungry, Norton dead. It
must have been difficult
explaining what happened
– most hawkward.

Famous Tudors

Francis Drake

Tudor explorers played an important part in finding new lands and bringing back exciting new things and riches to Britain. Sailing across stormy oceans was high risk, especially at a time when pirates were ready to rob any ship they saw. So here are a few short, sharp facts about Francis Drake, a famous Elizabethan:

Born: 1540s in Devon, England
Died: 1596 of dysentery in Panama. He was buried at sea, wearing his suit of armour and in a lead coffin. Divers have yet to find it. Drake was the first Englishman to sail around the world. After returning, he became a privateer – someone who attacked enemy ships (especially the Spanish) and stole their cargo. The Spanish saw him as a pirate, but to Queen Elizabeth I he was a hero, especially when he defeated the Spanish navy coming to attack England (the Armada of 1588).

Silly riddle

How many ears did Sir Francis Drake have?

Lots. A left ear, a right ear and a ship full of privateers.

Walter Raleigh

Another famous Tudor adventurer and explorer was born in 1554. He was also a firm favourite of Queen Elizabeth. He sailed to America and named the first English colony Virginia after Queen Elizabeth. He supposedly brought back tobacco and potatoes to England, but some historians question this.

Another story goes that Raleigh spread his cloak in front of Queen Elizabeth so that she didn't have to stand in a puddle. No wonder she liked him – or maybe she was just mad about his chips and cigarettes. After she died, he was sent to prison for 13 years accused of treason and he was beheaded. Apparently, his last words before his head was chopped off were to his executioner: 'Strike, man, strike!' Yep – he finally had his chips!

Limerick

Just how to pronounce Walter Raleigh?
It's usual to rhyme it with 'barley'
Though if you rhyme 'daily'
With the name Walter Raleigh,
You'll get laughed at and look a right Charlie.

William Shakespeare

The most famous writer of plays and poetry, and the inventor of English words, was another favourite of Queen Elizabeth. In fewer than 140 words, here's a quick reminder of his life:

 **1564** William Shakespeare was born in Stratford-upon-Avon.

Aged 18, he married Anne Hathaway, a farmer's daughter aged 26.  **1582**

 **1585** Despite having three children to look after, 21-year-old Shakespear left Stratford for London to start his career in the theatre.

1590s

He wrote many plays and sonnets even though plague closed London theatres.

68

1594 He set up the Lord Chamberlain's Men, an acting company.

The Globe Theatre opened in Southwark, south of the River Thames. Shakespeare was a part owner.

1599

1603

Queen Elizabeth I, an admirer of Shakespeare's plays, died.

1616

Shakespeare died after a fever at the age of 52. He was buried in Stratford-upon-Avon. Shakespeare remains the world's best-selling playwright, with sales of his plays and poetry reaching over four billion copies in the 400 years since his death.

Stink alert

Tudor theatres were smelly places, particularly in front of the stage where poorer people would stand in the rain, dirt and straw – known as the pit. These people were called 'groundlings' or 'penny stinkards' as their place was cheap but smelly. Rich people paid 12 pennies (one shilling) to sit on the stage or in special decorated boxes sheltered from the weather. Audiences were often rowdy as they shouted and clapped, laughed and booed. Sometimes they threw fruit, vegetables or anything at hand if they didn't like a character on the stage.

Gross alert

As theatres would have been infested with rats and fleas, itchy performances probably helped to spread diseases like the plague. Sneezy, sweaty, flea-ridden bodies packed together would be the breeding ground for germs. During Shakespeare's time, many theatres were closed to stop the plague from spreading. He had to concentrate more on writing than acting at such times. One of his famous plays that we can't mention because the name is said to bring bad luck (actually, it's *Macbeth* – oops) has a foul recipe mixed up by some witches. Try this for a delicious magic stew (you may find some of the ingredients at the local shop if you're lucky… or not!).

Witch's brew

Fillet of a fenny snake,
In the cauldron boil and bake;
Eye of newt and toe of frog,
Wool of bat and tongue of dog,
Adder's fork and blind-worm's sting,
Lizard's leg and howlet's wing,
For a charm of powerful trouble,
Like a hell-broth boil and bubble.
Cool it with a baboon's blood,
Then the charm is firm and good.

Delicious, but what's for pudding?

Talking of witches… the Tudors went over-the-top with worrying about them. The fear of magic, superstitions and wicked old women with black cats and broomsticks was crazy. Thousands of people were accused of witchcraft, then tortured and burnt to death.

Tudor witchery

People were convinced that all bad things were caused by witches. Anyone who suffered a hardship might blame someone living nearby for casting an evil spell. Witch hunts became a serious business. In 1542 new laws made witchcraft a crime that could be punished by death.

If a cow was ill, it must have been cursed. If plague came to a village, a witch must have caused it. If crops didn't grow, it must be a witch's fault. Anyone who owned a cat, a toad or a bird could be a suspect. Anyone with a wart on the nose, a hairy hand or an unusual birthmark might be arrested, especially old women living on their own. Anyone who boiled up home-made cures (probably most people!) could be accused of cooking up spells.

A common way to test if someone was a witch was to tie them to a ducking stool. Then they would be plunged under water in a pond or river. If the accused floated, she or he was declared a witch and burned to death. If not, they were innocent (and likely drowned anyway).

Cheesy witch riddles

Q. What is the problem with twin witches?
A. You never know which witch is which.

Q. What do you call a witch
   at the beach?
A. A sand-witch.

Q. How do you make a witch itch?
A. Take away her W.

Tudors were very superstitious and believed in all sorts of lucky charms or unlucky objects. Some Tudor superstitions are still found today.

- Don't walk under a ladder – they are bad luck because they are linked to gallows (the wooden frame for hanging people).

- Say 'Bless you' when someone sneezes – this is to stop the Devil entering your body through your open mouth.

- Don't spill salt – salt was very expensive in Tudor times, so spilling it was seen as very bad luck.

Have you ever seen old boots or shoes tied to the back of a car at a wedding? This custom probably came from Tudor times, when it was considered good luck for brides and grooms to have shoes hurled at them. Today we throw confetti instead, as it causes fewer bruises.

Punishments

Breaking Tudor laws (and there were plenty) could get you into serious trouble. Even a child who took a few birds' eggs from a noble's land could be hanged. If they were lucky not to be hanged, they might have a letter 'T' (for thief) burnt into their flesh with a red-hot iron. Beggars might be branded on the cheek with the letter 'V' (for vagrant). Some thieves (look away now if you're squeamish) had their nostrils slit and their ears or hands chopped off.

If you were starving and stole a crust of bread, you could be whipped. Many towns had a whipping post where a criminal would be chained and whipped for all to see as a warning.

Public

shame

The pillory was a T-shaped block of wood with holes to hold a criminal's hands and head. Anyone being punished would have to stand in this device in the middle of the market to be mocked and insulted by passers-by. Stocks were also used, but these held a person's feet. The stocks were a block of wood with two holes for the feet to be locked in. Local people threw rubbish and rotten eggs or bags of soot at anyone locked all day in the stocks for committing petty crimes.

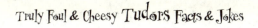

A punishment for women who were thought to have gossiped or spoken too much was the brank. This was a large iron frame put over the head like a cage. There was a metal strip on the brank that went into the woman's mouth and it was pointed or covered with sharp spikes. If the wearer tried to talk, she'd get her mouth stabbed. Ouch!

People who were caught drunk in public could be forced to wear a 'drunkard's cloak'. This was a large barrel with holes cut for the person's hands and head. The wearer then had to stagger around for all to see, with insults being hurled from everyone.

For more serious crimes, people could be
carted off to the Tower of London to be
tortured. Stretching people on the rack
would make them talk, before they were
slowly pulled limb from limb. Others might
be 'pressed' under heavy weights before
being crushed to death. Anyone blamed for
trying to murder someone could be boiled
alive in a big bowl of hot water.

Limerick

As a Tudor accused of a crime,
You would fear being boiled in your prime.
Getting hanged, drawn and quartered
Or publicly slaughtered,
Was such a bad use of your time.

Mad
medicine

The last time you had your haircut, did you think about asking the hairdresser to cut you deliberately? Believe it or not, Tudors often went to their barber to have bad teeth pulled out, boils popped or to be 'bled'. That's because they thought some illnesses were caused by having too much blood in the body. The answer was either to splat leeches (blood-sucking, worm-like creatures) all over the skin to drink blood, or to have a vein cut to let that extra blood drain away. Not a good idea if you're feeling poorly!

Tudors also thought diseases like plague
were spread by poisonous vapours or
smells, which drifted through the air
and were absorbed through the skin.
A bunch of nice smelling flowers or
petals in your lap would keep you safe.
Wrong! No one knew about germs then.

Rich Tudors might have been able to afford a doctor. If you felt ill, your doctor would ask you to wee in a bowl. By looking at its colour, sniffing and even tasting your wee, the doctor would decide how to treat you. It might mean a visit to the apothecary who used plants, herbs and all sorts of weird ingredients to make medicines.

This might kill you, but at least it will stop your hiccups.

How about these 10 bizarre Tudor remedies (best not try these at home):

 For headaches, drink a mixture of lavender, sage, marjoram, rose and rue (all herbs).

2 **If that fails, try pressing a hangman's rope to the head.**

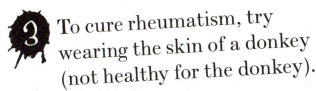

3 To cure rheumatism, try wearing the skin of a donkey (not healthy for the donkey).

4 A treatment for gout was to put a foul mixture on the foot – made from worms, pigs' marrow and herbs all boiled together with hair from a red-haired dog.

5 For deafness, 'the gall of a hare' was mixed with grease from a fox and popped into the ear.

6 For deadly smallpox, just hang red curtains around the bed.

It's very RASH of me, but I refused to pay an on the SPOT fine.

7 For jaundice swallow nine lice mixed with ale each morning. The lice and ale mixture should be swallowed for seven days.

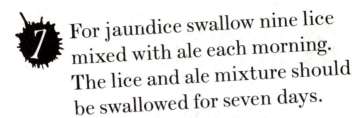

8 For breathing difficulties, swallow frogs greased with butter to help them slip down (although it could give you a cough or a frog in the throat!).

9 To stop baldness, smear the grease of a fox onto the scalp with crushed garlic and vinegar.

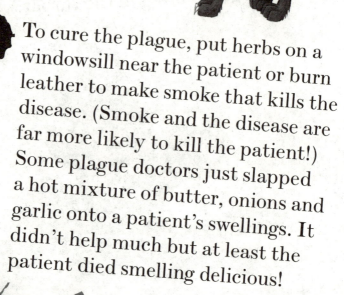

I'm going bald, but I still use a comb. I just can't part with it.

10 To cure the plague, put herbs on a windowsill near the patient or burn leather to make smoke that kills the disease. (Smoke and the disease are far more likely to kill the patient!) Some plague doctors just slapped a hot mixture of butter, onions and garlic onto a patient's swellings. It didn't help much but at least the patient died smelling delicious!

For the record

Diseases spread because of dirty conditions and plenty of toilet buckets being emptied into the streets.

Andreas Franciscius, an Italian visitor to London in 1497, was horrified by what he found and smelt. He was disgusted by the 'vast amount of evil-smelling mud' that covered the streets and lasted almost the whole year round.

97

Typhoid

This killer disease could be caught from food and water contaminated with bacteria from all that poo in the streets. It caused headaches, diarrhoea, weakness and horrible stomach pains. Typhoid usually started with a fever, but after several days of chronic diarrhoea, the victim would lose too much fluid and get very weak, and often their bowels would burst. Blood poisoning would follow, and then the major organs would shut down and they would die slowly. Drinking dirty water could be so risky that most people, including children, often drank beer with their meals, while the rich drank wine.

Toothache

The Tudors didn't have proper toothbrushes or toothpaste to keep their teeth clean. Some used toothpicks and tooth cloths to get rid of food in the mouth and to wipe their teeth. Even so, tooth decay could be a problem as it can lead to infections and poisoning. One mixture used to scrub teeth had a revolting ingredient (wait for it... **FOUL ALERT**) – mashed-up mouse heads. How about this recipe for mouse head tooth powder?

'First catch some mice. Cut off their heads. Cook them in a pan until they are burned. Pound them into a gritty powder. Then use the powder to clean your teeth.'

Minty mouthwash might taste nicer (and less mousy).

99

Towards the end of the Tudor period, many people began to get a sweet tooth. Sugar was expensive because it came from overseas, but as it became more common, some rich Tudors grew so fond of sweet food that their teeth rotted or went black. Black teeth were a sign you were successful!

Queen Elizabeth I had teeth that were black with decay and many of them fell out, which meant her speech could be difficult to understand at times. Although she loved sweets, Elizabeth was so frightened of seeing a dentist that a bishop had one of his own teeth pulled out in front of her to show that the pain wasn't too terrible (he must have been a good actor to hide his agony).

Sport

Tudor football wasn't like it is today. For a start, the ball was no more than a pig's bladder blown-up like a balloon, and the pitch could be huge. It could stretch for miles from one village to another. The only rule was to get the ball between the posts in any way you could.

Teams had many more than eleven players and they could pick up the ball, run with it and attack other players. Things could turn nasty and become a game of life and death. Football often got out of hand and ended up with players attacking each other or even killing someone.

A writer in Tudor times
described football like this:

'Football is more a fight than a
game... sometimes their necks are
broken, sometimes their backs,
sometimes their legs... football
encourages envy and hatred...
sometimes fighting, murder and a
great loss of blood.'

With such violent matches, young
men were at risk of getting injured
and not being able to fight for the
king or queen. In 1540, in the reign
of Henry VIII, football was banned.

John Tyler and Thomas Wylson (aged 15
and 16) both died playing football when one
fell heavily after tripping on a mole hill. The
other boy was accidentally stabbed in the
thigh by the knife in the belt of the player
he tackled. Health and safety rules had yet
to be invented.

Tudor timeline

 Henry VII is crowned
at Westminster Abbey –
the first Tudor king.

 Henry VII marries
Elizabeth of York, uniting
the two houses and ending
the Wars of the Roses.

 Bubonic plague kills
thousands of people in London.

105

 **1502**

Henry VII's son Arthur, Prince of Wales, dies, leaving his widow, Catherine of Aragon. His other son (11-year old Henry, Duke of York) becomes first in line to the throne.

 1509

Henry VII dies and is succeeded by his younger son Henry VIII. Two months later, King Henry VIII marries his brother's Spanish widow, Catherine of Aragon.

1528

Henry VIII asks the pope to end his marriage so that he can marry Anne Boleyn.

106

1533 Henry VIII marries Anne Boleyn, following his divorce from Catherine of Aragon. Anne Boleyn gives birth to Elizabeth in September.

1534 Henry VIII makes himself head of the Church of England.

1536 Henry VIII's second wife Anne Boleyn is executed. 11 days later he marries Jane Seymour.

1537 Prince Edward is born to Henry **VIII** and Jane Seymour. She dies shortly afterwards.

1540 Henry **VIII** marries Anne of Cleves but divorces her six months later to marry Catherine Howard (who is beheaded two years later).

1543 Henry **VIII** marries wife number six, Katherine Parr, who outlives him.

1545   France tries to invade England. Henry VIII's warship the *Mary Rose* sinks in Portsmouth Harbour – up to 500 sailors are killed.

Running the country is utter child's play!

1547   Henry VIII dies and is succeeded by nine-year-old Edward VI.

1553   Edward VI dies and is succeeded by Lady Jane Grey. Nine days later she is beheaded and replaced by Mary Tudor (Henry VIII's eldest daughter, known as Bloody Mary).

109

1554 Queen Mary marries Catholic King Philip II of Spain despite widespread opposition.

1558 Queen Mary dies. Henry VIII's daughter by Anne Boleyn is crowned Elizabeth I.

1570 Sir Francis Drake sets sail on his first voyage to the West Indies.

 1587 England and Spain are at war. Mary Queen of Scots is charged with plotting to kill Elizabeth I and is beheaded.

1589 Sir Francis Drake arrives at Plymouth after sailing all around the world.

1588 King Philip II of Spain sends an armada of ships to attack Britain but is defeated.

1590s

Shakespeare puts on his first plays in London. More plagues strike the capital.

1603 Queen Elizabeth I dies. King James of Scotland becomes the first Stuart king of England and the Tudor dynasty ends. He inherits a country in debt, but also hundreds of lovely royal dresses.

And finally...

... a spooky finish (please don't read this after dark or in bed late at night, just in case a Tudor ghost is watching...)

Why does the ghost of Anne Boleyn keep chasing the ghost of Henry VIII?
Answer: because she's trying to get ahead, while he still likes to chop and change.

Yes, Henry VIII's second wife, ever since meeting her gruesome end, has been 'seen' in many places. It seems Anne Boleyn is one of the most reported and most travelled Tudor ghosts. At Hampton Court, her sad ghost has apparently appeared dressed in dark blue or black, floating down the corridors. The Tower of London, the site of her execution, is full of ghostly stories – sometimes about the dead queen drifting through the night with her head tucked under her arm.

Anne's ghost is said to appear each Christmas at Hever Castle, her childhood home in Kent. She has been seen under a great oak tree where Henry VIII used to meet her. They say her ghost walks across the bridge on the castle grounds.

Fifty miles away, Anne's ghost has also been reported standing at the window in the Dean's Cloister at Windsor Castle. A legend claims her ghost has been seen running down a corridor, clutching her head and screaming. Maybe she'd met Henry's ghost searching for another wife!

Blickling Hall in Norfolk has a grisly Anne
Boleyn ghost story. On the anniversary of
her execution each year, she is said to arrive
dressed all in white, in a carriage drawn
by a headless coachman and four headless
horses, clutching her severed head. Eeek!
Not far away, a spooky tale tells that
Anne Boleyn was buried at Salle Church
in Norfolk, her body having been secretly
removed from the Tower of London. A
weird legend tells of her ghost turning into
a hare that leapt through the graveyard.
After all, hares were thought by Tudors
to be linked to witchcraft. Yikes – a really
hare-raising ghost story!

In Scotland, it seems the ghost of Mary Stuart (Mary Queen of Scots) pops up all over the place. Her ghost, known as the Pink Lady, is said to haunt Stirling Castle where she once lived, while the Green Lady is said to be her servant, who rescued Mary after a bedside candle set fire to her sheets.

- At Borthwick Castle, Midlothian, where Mary stayed in 1567 and escaped disguised as a man, she is meant to appear dressed as a page boy.
- Craignethan Castle near Lanark is apparently another haunt of Mary's headless ghost, where she stayed only briefly. She must have quit while she was ahead!
- The Palace of Holyroodhouse also has a spooky connection to Mary. A stain on the floor of her room is said to be the blood of her secretary David Rizzio, killed by order of her husband. They say the bloodstain has been scrubbed clean many times, only to reappear overnight. Ooer… don't have too many nightmares!

Final cheesy joke

Q: Which Tudor king was so weak
   in old age that he felt only a
   fraction of his former self?
A: Henry 1/8th

If you survived some of the truly foul
facts and cheesy jokes in this book, take
a look at the other wacky titles in this
revolting series. They're all guaranteed
to make you groan and squirm like
never before. Share them with your
friends **AT YOUR OWN RISK!**

QUIZ

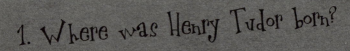

1. Where was Henry Tudor born?

a) A castle in Wales

b) A carpark in Kent

c) A palace in Scotland

2. Who was Henry Tudor's son?

a) Richard III

b) Henry VIII

c) Edward IX

3. Who was the Groom of the Stool?

a) Someone in charge of horse manure

b) The royal toilet cleaner

c) Someone who looked after the monarch's toiletry needs

4. What was Mary Tudor known as?

a) Mary Queen of Shops

b) Bloody Mary

c) Scary Mary of Scots

5. Which Tudor invention did John Harington invent?

a) A flushing water closet

b) A type of wrist clock

c) The first tennis racquet

6. How did Tudors test if someone was a witch?

a) Sprinkle them with salt

b) Dunk them in the river

c) Give them a blood test

7. Which of these was NOT a Tudor torture?

a) Tickling to death with a swan feather

b) Stretching arms and legs on a rack

c) Squashing the body under a heavy weight

8. Which of these was NOT a Tudor medicine?

a) Aspirin mixed with honey and lemon

b) Lice mixed with ale

c) Frogs greased with butter

9. Queen Elizabeth I was said to have which of these?

a) Green toe nails

b) Black teeth

c) Red eyes

10. Who was NOT a wife of Henry VIII?

a) Catherine Howard

b) Anne of Cleves

c) Catherine of Arrogant

Answers:
1 = a
2 = b
3 = c
4 = b
5 = a
6 = b
7 = a
8 = a
9 = b
10 = c

GLOSSARY

Arsenic: a very poisonous chemical, usually a white powder having no smell.

Bubonic plague: a deadly disease spread from fleas on rats, causing fever, weakness and black swellings.

Catholic Church: a branch of the Christian church with the Pope as its head.

Civil war: a war between opposing groups of citizens of the same country.

Dynasty: a series of rulers from the same family down the generations.

Privateer: a sailor on an armed private ship permitted by its government to make war on ships of an enemy country.

Protestant Church: a branch of the Christian church which was developed in the 16th century by Christians who disliked the Catholic Church.

Treason: the crime of trying to overthrow the government or ruler of a country.

INDEX

I finished reading this Truly
Foul & Cheesy book on:

........../........../..........